Estate to the Heart

How to plan wills and estates for your loved ones

Edward Olkovich

62 Jane Street
Toronto, Ontario
M6S 3Y4
416-769-9800
edo@mrwills.com

WARNING

This book provides general information on estate planning. The publisher and author are not providing legal, tax or professional advice or services and are not responsible for the result of any actions taken based on errors, omissions or information in this book. This book is not a substitute for professional help and is not intended to provide a basis for action without competent professional help. Laws change and this book cannot be considered a source or substitute for professional advice. The writer and publisher accept no responsibility or liability for risk and damage caused or alleged, directly or indirectly, to any person based on information in this book or its use.

Published by: Mr. Wills Inc. Toronto, Estatetips.com
Author: Olkovich, Edward, 1951–
Estate to the Heart – How to Plan Wills and Estates for Your Loved Ones.

ISBN# 0-9731588-0-8

Dear Reader:

"Home is where the heart is." -proverb

I have a plan to protect my loved ones. In this book, I will show how you can create your own plan.

Why do you need to plan? Traditional approaches to estate planning have made it feel like a chore you keep putting off. I want you to put your heart into it. I've covered the essential steps you need to follow so those closest to your heart benefit from your estate.

Regardless of your age or circumstances, your loved ones count on you to protect them. You may have children who need guardians assigned, and their education costs covered if something happens to you. Or you may have to help parents or children take care of their own affairs.

Whatever your situation, you will find *Estate to the Heart* gives you tips to unlock the mysteries of estate planning. With my approach, you can avoid costly errors and save taxes, time and money. You can start immediately to create or revise your estate plan.

Use my guide to protect those closest to your heart and you will be rewarded with peace of mind.

Ed "Mr. Wills" Olkovich
Lawyer and Author of *Estate Planning In Six Simple Steps for Canadians*
edo@MrWills.com

DEDICATION

To those closest to my heart, Krystyna, Nicholas and Adam Olkovich.

ACKNOWLEDGEMENTS

Many people must be thanked for helping produce this book. Chief among those who have laboured with me is my wife Krystyna. Her insights and suggestions always prove invaluable. Our dear friend, artist Jerzy Kolacz, provided the inspiration for the cover and title.

Many people reviewed parts of the manuscript, and I wish to thank Karen Rolfe for her editing skills. Lawyers, Milton Zwicker, Adam Cappelli and Glenn Stephens and Paul Truster offered helpful insights. Paul Barreca CFP and Bev Evans CFP; Jim Bullock, registrar at **www.peelinstitute.com** and my son Nicholas provided comments that were appreciated and triggered many improvements.

It is a privilege to work with individuals who are dedicated. Darlene Jukes, Eletra Lasci and Patricia Standello have made a difference helping me with the manuscript and my law practice.

Editorial: Karen Rolfe
Design: The ArtAffairs Group
Cover: Jerzy Kolacz
Art: Jerzy Kolacz

CONTENTS

"Knowledge is of two kinds; we know a subject ourselves, or we know where we can find information upon it." - Samuel Johnson

FOREWORD

Introduction – Your benefits from reading *Estate to the Heart*

Take Action – Protect your loved ones

Identify Assets - Learn your ownership rights

Preview Debts - You can reduce taxes

Make Wills - Choose executors, beneficiaries and guardians

Protect Yourself – Use powers of attorneys and trusts

Consider Extras – Insurance, business and executor's work

Review Changes - Revise and record

FOREWORD

Estate to the Heart is a catchy title for a book, but the words contain this wisdom: Estate planning is more about love than it is about money and mortality. It's a way to show you care for those you love and the things you value.

Love is easier to display than it is to define. A well crafted will is a part of your plan, a good way to show you care. You should operate on the assumption that your family structure will alter after your death and may turn into a civil war among your remaining family members. A will at least establishes the rules of engagement.

Estate planning covers a broad spectrum of choices that range from who controls your bank account should you be incapacitated, to who decides where to bury your remains. That's why the idea that one size fits all is silly. Do-it-yourself kits are symbols of a bad idea. How can one size fit every situation? The elderly who face the frightening prospect of limbo, between competence and death need unique solutions. An ever-changing array of non-traditional families and other close personal relationships call for their own unique solutions.

Estate to the Heart has questionnaires and checklists to help you explore your values, feelings and objectives about estate planning issues. You need to know what options are available and this knowledge gives you power. In pages that follow you can explore many estate planning options and how to exercise them.

Many people put off planning their estates believing it can wait for another day. How do you know you have another day?

At what point in your life do you stop thinking about yourself and start pondering the futures of others - those you love. Many wealthy people leave a legacy of money to their favourite charities but you too can leave a legacy - a legacy of love - your choice.

Milton W. Zwicker, B Comm., LLB.,
Estate Planner and author of *Developing & Management a Successful Law Firm* and *Successful Client Newsletters* : *The Complete Guide to Creating Powerful Newsletters.*

INTRODUCTION

Your benefits from reading *Estate to the Heart*

*"I shall the effect of this good lesson keep.
As watchman to my heart."* - William Shakespeare

"Estate Sale." What do you think of when you see these words? You probably expect to get a bargain. Unfortunately, there's some truth in that. As a lawyer, I see families selling assets to pay bills, taxes or to support themselves. However, if you plan now, you can avoid an estate sale regardless of your financial status or age.

Estate planning is not only for the wealthy. Think of your estate as another word for your loved ones, the family, friends, pets and causes that need your protection. Estate to the Heart will help you provide for them after you die.

TIPS TO PLANNING

I can show you how to take the first important steps to set your goals and then take action. My simple approach will give you the techniques to take command of your planning. Each section of my book consists of three chapters with **Definitions** and **Estate Tips** to help you understand estate planning terms.

After working through this book you can use your research to save time with your estate planning professionals so together you can reach your planning goals.

Throughout your life your needs will change. As you start a job, have a family, acquire assets or become ill, you'll need to update your plan.

ESTATE TO THE HEART BENEFITS

1. **You will make better wills**
   Avoid traps, tricks and troubles and going to court over your will.

2. **You will save income and probate taxes**
   Preview your estate to reduce taxes without risk.

3. **You will find the right person for every job**
   Compare roles for executors, trustees and attorneys.

4. **You will understand powers of attorney, living wills and personal care issues**
   Appoint persons you trust to decide if you cannot.

5. **You will learn the tax-free advantages of life insurance**
   Provide for your family and achieve your estate goals.

6. **You will learn how to use trusts to secure assets**
   Protect children, or those persons with special needs.

7. **You will protect yourself in marriage or divorce**
   Get advice for when you marry, separate or divorce.

8. **You will benefit from legal checkups**
   Use reminders and checklists to review estate plans.

9. **You will learn how you settle an estate**
   What to expect as executor or beneficiary.

10. **You will prepare asset and document inventories**
    Provide essentials for loved one's peace of mind.

I see families torn apart when relatives get bad advice or none at all. You own it to yourself and your loved ones to make sure no one will take advantage of them.

Every adult needs to understand the essentials of estate planning to prevent unnecessary tragedies. You can use this information to protect the hearts and homes of those you love. After you finish this book, you will need to invest in experience professional advice. Don't put everything at risk and gamble by doing it yourself.

DEFINITIONS

Estate – whatever you leave behind when you die, includes your assets and liabilities. Think of estate as another word for your loved ones whom you want to benefit with your estate.

Will – legal document you sign to deal with your estate after you die. Your executors distribute your estate to beneficiaries.

Powers of attorney – legal documents to designate agents to handle your finances or health care decisions while you are alive.

Estate tip: Estate to the Heart will save money and protect loved ones.

12

TAKE ACTION

PROTECT YOUR LOVED ONES.

Young or old, rich or poor, you need a plan. Remember, without taking action, your good intentions are worthless and besides, who will do it if you don't?

CHAPTER ONE

THE HEART OF THE MATTER

"Riches are gotten with pain, kept with care and lost with grief."
- proverb

Let's get right to the point. *Estate to the Heart* helps you avoid problems. Estate planning puts you in charge of what happens to your estate. People always say "I want my money to go straight to my loved ones." Picture it looking like this:

Estate to the Heart is what you do to ensure that your hard-earned money goes to those closest to your heart. Detours bite into your estate with unnecessary legal costs, taxes and delays.

You buy a home, invest or start a business to provide for yourself and your family. What will happen if you die or become incapacitated by illness? You have to take one more step to plan for these realities. Taking care of this responsibility will give you tremendous peace of mind. Of course without actions, good intentions are worthless and will only lead you into trouble.

PLANNING FOR LOVED ONES

I want you to start planning with one simple idea: if you don't take the time to protect your loved ones, who will? You want to provide for your family, friends and causes so they will benefit from your estate.

Take a moment to list the people who benefit from your planning. This will motivate you to take action.

My loved ones include: ....

Do you have a list of other individuals to protect? List them here:

Don't forget charities, your favourite causes and pets:

Planning needs clear objectives to be effective so in the next chapter you will get a chance to be specific about your goals for the people you love.

If you already have an estate plan, then take this quiz to see how healthy it is.

ESTATE PLAN CHECKUP

Are your loved ones at risk because your estate plan is incomplete?
Use this checkup to make sure your estate plan is in good health.

Circle your answer.

My loved ones know where my up-to-date will is stored.	**yes**	**no**	**unsure**
I have backup executors and guardians for minor children in my will.	**yes**	**no**	**unsure**
I have legally appointed someone to handle decisions for me if I cannot.	**yes**	**no**	**unsure**
I have a strategy in place to save probate and income taxes.	**yes**	**no**	**unsure**
I have provided for loved ones with special needs.	**yes**	**no**	**unsure**
I have a plan to deal with my business if I die.	**yes**	**no**	**unsure**
I regularly preview my estate plan to ensure that it achieves my goals.	**yes**	**no**	**unsure**
I review my loved ones' needs so my estate protects them.	**yes**	**no**	**unsure**
I have an updated inventory of assets and valuable documents.	**yes**	**no**	**unsure**
My life and disability insurance coverage will replace income, cover taxes and gifts.	**yes**	**no**	**unsure**

 Estate tip: No one should go through life without planning for their loved ones.

CHAPTER TWO

SET PERSONAL GOALS

"A goal is a dream that has an ending." - Duke Ellington

You need to set goals. Without them you have no direction and will likely go around in circles. *Estate to the Heart* gives you a roadmap to reach your destination.

One common example of failing to plan is not making a will. If you die without a will you cannot decide who inherits your estate; provincial laws dictate who gets what. Your wishes are disregarded and loved ones can suffer as their real needs are ignored.

Planning identifies your personal estate goals and helps you reach them. Perhaps you want to leave money for a child's education or for your university's scholarship fund? Or you may need to set aside money to protect a disabled partner or young children through a trust fund. What you want to accomplish for yourself and loved ones is unique and there aren't any comprehensive solutions that come in a box.

LEGAL AND MORAL OBLIGATIONS

Can you do whatever you want with your estate? The short answer is no. Certain laws can prevent you from doing whatever you want. When you set goals, you cannot, for example, ignore someone's legal rights. Here is what I mean.

Your married spouse has a legal right to share in your estate. Each province has property and support laws to protect married spouses. Common-law and same-sex partners, your dependents and children have similar legal rights that can be enforced in court.

In some cases you have no legal obligations to cover when planning. You may however want to give something back to your community, fund medical research or leave a gift to charity. You may feel this as a moral obligation.

START NOW

Take a moment to outline your estate goals. Make a random list and do not worry about your priorities or specifics at this point. Here is a sample:

1. I want to travel without worrying about my family.

2. I want to help my partner manage if I have a sudden accident.

3. I need to take care of my kids, stepchildren and charities.

4. I want control over my own care and money if I develop health problems.

YOUR PERSONAL GOALS

This is where you decide what your personal goals are.
Write them down here.

_____

_____

_____

_____

Now is a good time for your partner (if you have one) to make his
or her own list.

_____

_____

_____

_____

It's normal to have different goals from your partner.

ASSET GOALS

You may wish to deal with specific assets. Here is where you identify key property like a business, heirlooms or a beneficiary's request.

_____

_____

_____

_____

QUESTIONS TO ASK ADVISORS

If you need help with specific goals or assets use this space to list your questions.

_____

_____

_____

_____

ESTATE PLAN ASSESSMENT

Look at estate planning as an ongoing process as part of keeping your financial house in order. Do you already have a will or other estate documents in place? Now is a good time to dig them out for a checkup.

Collect any of the following that you may have or take time to prepare them. Make copies of important documents like marriage and birth certificates and government benefits you receive. If you don't already have them, you'll find some lists set out in the appendix to help you.

Asset Inventory – lists all your property and where it can be found

Ownership Documents – real estate deeds, bank and business investments

Designations – pensions, life insurance and RRSPs or RRIFs

Insurance Policies – life, disability, health, car and property

Debt Inventory – list your payment obligations and documents

Will – for you and your partner, record where the originals are stored

Powers of Attorney – finances and health care in duplicate

Funeral Arrangements – preferences for services and burial

Now that you have the details of your estate and have outlined your goals, you need to focus on who can help you reach them.

 Estate tip: Your estate planning documents must reflect changes in your goals.

CHAPTER THREE

GET HELP

"Believe one who has proved it. Believe an expert." – Virgil

Do you start estate planning with your financial advisor, accountant or lawyer? It does not matter as long as you start. Experts will point you in the right direction and show you how to get results. *Estate to the Heart* will help you understand and clarify your professional advisor's role.

At different life stages you may need help from some or all of the following professionals:

- **Financial Advisors** to provide licensed financial planning and investment advice

- **Life insurance professionals** to ensure that you can provide support and cover your needs

- **Estate planning lawyers** to plan and prepare documents to carry out your estate plan

- **Tax advisers/accountants** to preview and reduce tax liability

- **Trust officers** to set up trusts or administer estates with trust companies

Don't put your loved ones at risk with amateurs. Remember, use professionals who are competent, compatible and certified. Consider professional advice as an investment that pays you back and not as an expense. Get referrals from friends and work with people you trust enough to invite to dinner.

QUESTIONS TO ASK EVERY PROFESSIONAL ADVISOR:

1. Are you paid on a flat rate, hourly or commission basis?

2. Do you require a minimum-size estate or fee to get started?

3. What qualifications, licenses or certifications do you have?

4. How many years of experience do you have with my type of case?

5. If something is wrong with our relationship, what can happen?

DOING-IT-YOURSELF DANGERS

Perhaps you prepare your own tax returns. If you make mistakes Ottawa charges you interest and penalties. If you deliberately cheat, you can even go to jail. Do not try this with your estate because no one knows you made a mistake until after your death. Lawyers and judges cannot fix your mistakes if you get sloppy, but relatives may waste thousands of dollars trying. So will you pay now or pay later?

ESTATE PLAN CHECKUP

Here is a quick quiz to help you find out why you need professional help. Circle your answer.

CAN YOU PROTECT YOURSELF?

Are you doing it yourself because you think you can't afford help?   **yes / no**

Good professional advice comes in all price ranges. Find advice to suit your budget.

Do you feel doing it yourself is better than nothing?   **yes / no**

Henry did his own will and left everything to his wife, or so he thought. He left out one sentence and actually left his estate to charity.

Are you insured for a mistake?   **yes / no**

Legislation and court decisions change the law every day. Licensed professionals are insured and maintain high standards with ongoing education.

Are there any silent victims? **yes / no**

Do you realize that you are dragging your family members into the problem? When you are gone, they will have to pick up the pieces.

Have you received a second opinion? **yes / no**

If you have done it yourself, have your handiwork checked by professionals. You will be doing everyone a favour.

Don't you want to make a professional investment? **yes / no**

Good advice pays dividends over a long time. Well-drafted, professional wills can serve your needs for ten years. When you average the cost, it is pennies a day for protection.

You will clarify your goals and achieve realistic results with professional help. The next tip to planning is to understand what your estate looks like.

Estate tip: No one should go through life without planning for their loved ones.

IDENTIFY ASSETS

LEARN YOUR OWNERSHIP RIGHTS.

Your assets – the things you own may one day belong to your heirs. How you own things affects how you can transfer property to your loved ones.

CHAPTER FOUR

SLICE UP YOUR ESTATE

"The money that men make lives after them". – Samuel Butler

Draw a circle. Imagine it contains your estate assets. Now divide the circle into three wedges. These three wedges represent three kinds of assets in your estate: joint, designated and will assets.

When you die these assets are controlled respectively by laws, contracts and wills. It's important to remember that each asset group has distinct ownership characteristics with different planning consequences.

1. Joint Assets

Your home and bank account, jointly owned with your partner, are examples of joint assets. Joint owners have the rights of survivorship law. This means joint assets pass on death to the surviving owner. You cannot control joint assets by your will.

2. Designated Assets

Your RRSPs, RRIFs, life insurance and pension plans have designated beneficiaries. Such assets are transferred after your death by written designation to your named beneficiaries.

3. Will Assets

Anything not designated or jointly owned as part of the other two wedges is covered by your will.
Note: Life insurance policies or assets made payable to your estate are will assets.

Each asset slice in your circle may be a different size. Whether your pie is thousands or millions of dollars, everything you own fits into one of these sections. Understanding how these assets affect your estate is a key to planning. We will look at all three in turn, starting with the simplest, to understand your will assets.

WILL ASSETS

If assets are in your name only, you are the sole owner. These are will assets and are controlled by your will. At your death the estate transfers these assets by will. Without a will, the government dictates how your will assets are to be divided on your death and your wishes are irrelevant.

Will assets include cars, houses, shares and bank accounts among other things. Your will slice could be a very small portion of your overall estate. Even if it is small, you still need a will.

The size of your will assets can change. For example, you might inherit property from another joint owner or designated beneficiary who dies first. These assets would be part of your will estate even if they are inherited or received after you sign your will. Planning always deals with such contingencies so that you won't have to frequently redo your will.

Do you own assets that are registered in your name or solely owned by you? Make a list as part of your asset inventory. Your grandfather's pocket watch, your jewelry, or your car are examples of will assets. These items usually are not controlled by separate contract or law and should be transferred to a beneficiary by will.

If you have no will or estate plan, government rules dictate who gets what of your estate. But planning is more than just making a will. As you'll see in the next chapter, joint ownership has features that everyone should consider for their loved ones.

DEFINITIONS

Probate – a process to prove who shares and administers your estate. Probate or estate courts control estates when someone dies with or without wills. Probate taxes are collected (except in Quebec) when probate papers are issued by a court.

Getting Probate – going through the probate process when someone dies. Estate courts supervise what happens to estates and confirm your executor or estate trustee.

Probate dispute – if you die without a will, judges decide who your estate legal representatives are. If your will is contested, it cannot be accepted for probate until a court settles the dispute. Loved ones wait and pay for the delay.

 Estate tip: Estates contain three types of property: joint, designated and will assets.

CHAPTER FIVE

JOINT SURVIVORS

"What will survive us is love". – Philip Larkin

Let's look at the joint assets in your estate. Jointly owned assets come with special legal survivorship rights. This simplifies estate costs as these assets are automatically transferred on death without probate.

Joint owners must have survivorship rights expressly stated for the right to exist. For example, bank account application forms usually contain a statement confirming that they are joint. Emily and her daughter Vanessa jointly own Hardware Inc on a 50/50 basis. They each own 50 shares but there is no registration of joint ownership with survivorship. If Emily dies, her shares will not pass to Vanessa. Since Emily wants her shares to go to her daughter, she must ensure that they are registered as joint owners.

REAL ESTATE OWNERSHIP

Your title deeds to real estate can record joint ownership rights. Usually owners are recorded as "joint tenants" and not as "tenants in common." Joint owners of real estate are called joint tenants even though they are owners and they have survivorship rights by law. The last to survive inherits even without a will.

Not everyone who owns real estate is, however, a joint owner. In a second marriage, for example, spouses may not own their principal residence as joint tenants. As well, many individuals who are not related hold assets as tenants in common. In this case, there is no right of survivorship on the death of the other owner.

Here's an example to clarify. Marco and his brother Anthony own a rental property. Marco paid 75 percent of the purchase price and Anthony put down 25 percent. Title deeds show this registered ownership:

Marco as to a 75 percent interest and Anthony as to a 25 percent interest as tenants in common.

DIVISION PROBLEMS OF JOINT ASSETS

Owning assets jointly with spouses reduces probate costs and is a valuable estate planning technique. But if all your assets are jointly owned, it may be impossible to treat beneficiaries equally. For example, Mark has a ski chalet jointly owned with his daughter. Mark wants to be fair and treat his son equally so he has registered his home in joint ownership with his son. Mark figures the two pieces of real estate have the same current value and that this is a fair division of his estate.

If Mark got professional advice he would be aware of certain issues. His personal residence could appreciate more quickly than the recreational property which will also receive different tax treatment on Mark's death. The result can be an unequal split between the two children and a legacy of painful planning.

JOINT OWNERSHIP RISKS

Joint ownership even with family can create legal problems. Here are five dangers that you must be aware of. Review this list before you consider holding property in joint ownership with anyone including children.

1. DISASTER

Joint owners can refuse to cooperate when you need to deal with the property.

2. DEATH

Your child could die first, or at the same time, which means you must plan for other contingencies.

3. DIVORCE

Divorced spouses of a child can make a claim to the property.

4. DEBTS

Creditors of bankrupt children can make claims against property.

5. DISPOSITION

Transfers of some assets can create a capital gain and other expenses.

Always discuss with your lawyer the advantages and disadvantages of having jointly owned assets. Consider the risks carefully before you give up control of your assets. Once someone is a joint owner, you can't remove him or her as a joint owner without that person's consent. If consent is not forthcoming, you could end up in a court fight.

Review probate in Chapter 9 before deciding what to hold jointly. Remember, you can't give away jointly owned property by your will unless the other joint owner dies first. You cover these assets in your will only in case the other joint owner dies first.

List jointly owned assets in your asset inventory (see appendix). Now you are ready to move on to identifying the special benefits of designated assets.

Estate tip: Joint ownership of assets with your spouse saves probate costs.

CHAPTER SIX

BE SURE TO DESIGNATE

"It isn't that they can't see the solution. It is that they can't see the problem."- G.K. Chesterton

Your third slice of estate pie has named beneficiaries. You designate beneficiaries with written designations usually as part of a contract. Life insurance, pension benefits or RRSPs or RIFs are common examples of assets with designated beneficiaries. After your death, designated beneficiaries receive benefits without complicated legal procedures. Usually, producing a death certificate and filling out a form can satisfy contract formalities to collect money.

Here's how it works. Moya wants her daughter Nichelle to get her life insurance benefits. She designated Nichelle as her beneficiary through her life insurance broker. Her life insurance proceeds now pass to her daughter outside her will and without probate. Moya does not have to deal with the policy in her will except as a contingency in case Nichelle dies first.

What if Nichelle is a minor when Moya dies? In that case, the life insurance proceeds would be paid into court. Moya may want to have life insurance controlled by her executor so she could make the policy payable to her estate. Her executor would then deal with her insurance proceeds according to her will.

BENEFITS OF DESIGNATION

The general rule would be to record your loved ones as direct beneficiaries for any designated assets in your estate pie. On your death these assets pass directly to your beneficiary without having the assets pass through probate, which saves time and money.

If you are single, you can designate your estate as a beneficiary unless you have creditors who can make first claim to these funds. If you have multiple beneficiaries you are better off dividing assets equally by your will. It is not practical to name all of your beneficiaries on every designated asset. You may also want to deal with the asset in a different way if a beneficiary dies before you. Your will is the place to deal with these contingencies.

CHANGING BENEFICIARIES IS EASIER

Life insurance beneficiaries, for example, can change to keep pace with your goals. When your children are young, your plan may be to use insurance to support them. You can designate the proceeds to go to their other parent or guardians. When children are older, your extra insurance coverage can fund major gifts to charitable causes, which will give you added tax credits after your death.

Peggy wants certain family heirlooms to go to her grandchildren when she dies. Are these items considered legally designated? Not unless there is a written and binding will or contract that someone can legally enforce. Designation can also help avoid any claims by creditors and estate expenses, which are covered in the next chapter.

DON'T FORGET TAXES

Remember some of your designated assets carry hidden tax consequences. Your planning should take advantage of any tax rules to save money. Small things can make a big difference when it comes to taxes as Scott's children discovered. For example, Scott had designated Kelly, the children's stepmother, as a beneficiary of his RRSP. After his divorce, Scott forgot to remove Kelly as his beneficiary. When Scott passed away, his savings fund was worth $100,000. Guess what? Kelly got the money. That's right, all of it. And Scott's children got the tax bill for the RRSPs.

Scott's estate had to include $100,000 from his RRSP as income in Scott's last tax return. His children inherited their father's estate under his will but they also got the tax bill. Although Scott wanted to leave his estate to his children, his oversight meant this wouldn't happen.

LET'S REVIEW

1. Your will must cover contingencies in case of the prior or simultaneous death of joint owners and designated beneficiaries.

2. Wills control the "will slice" of your estate pie. This might be only a small part of your total estate pie but it is important.

3. Jointly owned assets pass to the surviving joint owner without probate. The same goes for legally designated assets if your estate is not your designated beneficiary. This reduces costs so your estate goes to the people you care about.

Your executor uses your will assets to pay your bills. In the next section, Preview Debts, we will look at estate expenses and taxes. You will be surprised by what is covered in your final accounting.

 Estate tip: You can change beneficiaries on designated assets easily and without cost.

PREVIEW DEBTS

YOU CAN REDUCE TAXES.

You are a Canadian so you don't have to
worry about inheritance taxes when you
die. Canadians do have to pay provincial
probate taxes and income taxes though.
Learn how to enjoy the pleasures of paying
as little tax as possible.

CHAPTER SEVEN

ESTATE PREVIEWS

"Speak not of my debts unless you meant to pay them".
– Herbert 1651

Your beneficiaries hope your estate assets are greater than your estate liabilities. You can check this with a preview of your estate debts.

It's important to understand how estate expenses and debts are paid. Your designated beneficiaries or joint owners do not usually pay estate expenses. Only your will assets are used for this purpose. When we talk about liabilities, you will see that dying makes a difference. Some estate costs and debts are not encountered until after you're gone.

ESTATE EXPENSES

Estate expenses can ruin your expectations for the distribution of your estate. In some cases you may need life insurance to pay creditors so your loved ones won't suffer.

Here are four expenses that appear in most estates:

1. FUNERAL EXPENSES

If you do not prepay these, your estate ends up doing it. You can budget $10,000 to $15,000 or more.

2. EXECUTOR FEES

Executors or estate trustees are the people who handle your estate after you die. They pay bills, distribute your estate and can collect a fee. As a rule of thumb their compensation can be roughly five percent of your estate. Relatives may choose not to charge fees because they are beneficiaries and the fees are taxable.

Trust companies acting as your executors have you sign their compensation agreements in advance. Executor fees are paid after judge or beneficiary approval is received.

3. PROBATE TAXES

Executors need legal help to probate your estate. In Ontario, "getting letters probate" is now called applying for a "certificate of appointment." At that time, your estate pays probate taxes. Probate taxes vary from province to province.

4. LEGAL FEES

Lawyers help executors sell and distribute estate assets. You need to budget two to three percent of your will estate as a guideline for probate taxes and legal services.

IN SUMMARY

Up to ten percent of your "will" assets can be spent to cover estate expenses once executor fees are factored into the calculation. You can save money just by choosing family to handle this responsibility.

PREVIEW YOUR MAJOR DEBTS

Unless your estate is bankrupt, you cannot avoid tax or mortgage obligations by dying. Preview your estate to ensure you have assets to cover spousal support or a child's education costs. If you are not covered, you can reduce debt or purchase insurance.

Here's a list of possible debts:

- Mortgages, credit cards, guarantees
- Loans: personal, bank, car, family
- Business debts and government liabilities
- Support obligations by contract or court order
- Unrealized capital gains on real estate or business assets

The biggest bill most of us will pay is the final income tax bill, which will be reviewed in the next chapter.

TAXES ARE PAID FIRST

Can you avoid paying your taxes if you give away all your property before you die? It's a great idea, but it won't make your tax bill disappear because Ottawa will not give up all that revenue. When you make a gift of capital property before you die you have to report any capital gains and pay income tax.

Your joint or designated assets can also generate tax bills for your estate. Usually only assets controlled by your will are available to pay bills. Invest in professional advice to estimate your tax liability at death and that professional will show you ways to reduce taxes.

Do you think you are paying your fair share of taxes? Wait till you see what is coming next. Income tax bills can jump up and take a big bite out of your estate. If you are careful you can save money by planning ahead.

CHAPTER EIGHT

NO TAXES? NO WAY!

"The difference between death and taxes is that death never gets worse". – Anonymous

Like it or not, Ottawa is a beneficiary or partner in every estate. However, you can pay less tax and leave more for your loved ones. I will show you that in a moment but first you need to know these three fundamental tax concepts:

1. **DEEMED DISPOSITIONS** create income tax liability on some of your assets ate death

2. **TAX ROLLOVERS** provide advantageous tax deferrals when you transfer assets to qualifying beneficiaries

3. **TAX EXEMPTIONS** exist for assets you own like life insurance or your personal residence

Income, not your estate, is taxed.

In Canada, our income tax system collects taxes on income. We do not have an American-style inheritance tax on your overall estate. On death, income has an expanded definition and assets get different treatment for tax purposes. Your RRSPs, RRIFs, and undeclared capital gains in a business or investments, for example, can generate income. Your executor must report this income in your final tax return.

TAX RULES EVERYONE NEEDS TO KNOW

When you die, Ottawa has a way to collect income taxes. It considers that you disposed of all your property at fair market value. Ottawa taxes any increase in value of assets as if you sold them.

This is what the government calls a deemed disposition. Even if you give away assets and get nothing back, you still get a tax bill because of the deemed disposition rules.

Here are seven deadly tax rules you must know:

SEVEN DEADLY TAX RULES

1. DEEMED DISPOSITIONS – these tax rules force you to include all unrealized capital gains as income. Even if you do not get the actual sale proceeds, your estate pays income tax from your estate. Remember that executors may have access only to the assets covered by your will.

2. TERMINAL RETURN - your estate representative files your last tax return called your terminal tax return. It includes all income and capital gains. Certain income receives different tax treatment and, in some cases, filing separate tax returns can save money.

3. ESTATE TAX RETURNS – any income earned after death is reported by your estate, which files a separate tax return called a trust return.

4. TAX ROLLOVERS – use these to plan your estate distribution and to get tax deferrals. Assets with tax consequences should be left to your spouse to avoid deemed disposition rules. Spouses or a minor child can inherit RRSPs or RRIFs with tax-deferred transfers. Financially dependant grandchildren can also qualify.

5. TAX EXEMPT ASSETS – your principal residence can be transferred free of tax. You can designate only one home as your principal residence. Get advice to maximize tax credits. Life insurance benefits are also usually tax-free. These two assets can be used to benefit loved ones.

6. TAX CREDITS – donations to registered charities or the Crown can generate non-refundable tax credits. You can use credits to offset any taxes you owe at death. Consider gifts of cash, insurance, RRSPs, stocks or stock options as well.

7. PERSONAL LIABILITY – executors are personally responsible to pay income taxes from your estate assets. Executors distribute assets only after they obtain tax clearance certificates from the government.

Preview your estate tax liability with a professional to find ways to reduce taxes. You can do this with probate taxes, as you will see in the next chapter.

DEFINITIONS

Deemed Disposition - at death you are deemed to have received fair market value (FMV) proceeds for all capital property. It is deemed sold even if your estate gets no actual sale proceeds, only a tax liability. Capital property includes real estate, stocks, art and investments, but not cash.

Captial Gains – the difference between FMV and an asset's purchase cost may result in a gain or loss. Currently one-half of gains are reported as income on your final or terminal tax return.

Tax Rollovers – provide a tax deferral by avoiding the deemed disposition rules on capital property left to a spouse or a spousal trust. Some assets like insurance proceeds and one principal residence are both free from tax.

Estate tip: Use tax rollovers whenever possible to defer income tax paid by your estate.

CHAPTER NINE

PROBATE PERPLEXED?

Probate – from the Latin verb probare, to prove

What is probate? Many people have problems understanding probate, perhaps because it is a process as well as a tax, which has been around for centuries. Probate or estate courts must certify who represents you and who will share in your estate. This is important because many institutions refuse to transfer your assets to executors without court confirmation.

Provincial governments (except Quebec) charge different rates of probate taxes on the value of assets passing through your estate, whether you have a will or not.

Probate taxes are not the biggest problem you want to avoid by planning. Income tax rates are much higher and can equal 50 percent of your income. Boris's probate tax on his $100,000 RRSP is roughly $1500. The income tax liability in comparison can be $50,000. What do you think Boris should worry about?

PROBATE TAXES ARE LEGAL

Probate taxes are legal, and Ontario has the highest provincial rate at roughly $1,500 per $100,000 of your estate. You can reduce probate taxes by making gifts to lower the size of your probate estate. Designated and joint assets are not included in Ontario probate calculations. You can achieve savings simply by changing designated beneficiaries and holding assets jointly with rights of survivorship.

Here's how Carlos previewed and reduced his probate costs:

1. House (in Carlos' name alone) $250,000
2. RRSP (payable to his estate) $100,000
3. Life insurance (payable to his estate) $100,000
4. Bank term deposit (in his name only) $ 50,000

Total probate estate $ 500,000 @ $1500 per $100,000 = $7,500

Carlos rearranged his asset ownership. He became joint owners of his home with his spouse, Marian. He also designated Marian to be his life insurance beneficiary. When Carlos died, all his assets passed by designation or by rights of survivorship outside of his will estate. He was able to save his loved ones the probate taxes of $7,500 plus legal costs and potential executor fees as well.

COMMON-LAW SPOUSES

Common-law spouses do not automatically inherit your property in Ontario as the law currently stands in 2002. Each province has different family property laws that affect same-sex and common-law partners. These individuals may not inherit unless they are named in a will. Let's look at Lisa, whose common-law spouse Patrick would not receive anything if Lisa left no will. What if Lisa leaves the house to Patrick by her will?

If Patrick inherits the property under Lisa's will, her estate pays the probate taxes. Lisa's home is worth $300,000, and the probate tax would be roughly $4,500 in Ontario. This doesn't include the legal cost of obtaining probate, real estate appraisals and costs to transfer the property. Patrick estimated these costs to be around $8,000 to put the house he figured he owned into his name. Lisa could also have recorded Patrick as a joint owner of the home and saved this money for Patrick.

MULTIPLE WILLS

In some cases you can reduce probate by having multiple wills. Yes, you can have more than one will. It's a complex arrangement that requires experienced legal help. You can take advantage of this, for example, if you have a family corporation with substantial assets. You will want the corporate assets to pass to family members under your first will to your family. These assets will not be subject to probate tax if the will is not filed for probate.

Your first will deals only with assets that don't require probate to be transferred. You make a second will to cover your other public assets, which must not revoke your first one, and includes only assets that must be submitted for probate. Banks, for example, require court certificates to transfer assets.

Probate costs can be a necessary evil in estate planning. You can be better off in most cases keeping control of your own property as long as possible. If you give away all your assets too early just to avoid probate, you may find out too late that you need them.

LET'S REVIEW

1.   If your debts exceed your assets, plan on getting life insurance or dying broke.

2. Preview tax, probate and total estate expenses to see what you can distribute to beneficiaries.

3. You may want to keep control over your assets until death. Probate taxes may be the price your estate pays for this.

Now you can look at making wills, picking your executors and beneficiaries all of which are covered in the next section.

Estate tip: You can create problems by trying too hard to avoid probate taxes.

MAKE WILLS

**CHOOSE BENEFICIARIES, EXECUTORS
AND GUARDIANS.**

Learn the seven deadly sins to avoid when
making your will and how to chose the best
executors and guardians.

CHAPTER TEN

WILLS MADE EASY

"Wills are cornerstones on which you build". – E. Olkovich

Everyone needs a will. Wills absolutely save time and money in even small estates. You get to choose who benefits and controls your estate. You will be in command of your estate plan and can add guardians for minor children, create trusts and reduce taxes and grief.

Dying without a will creates problems. Your spouse does not automatically inherit your entire estate. In some provinces, you need to make a will for children, common-law or same-sex spouse to inherit anything. Until a court appoints an estate trustee, loved ones must wait. If you are lucky, your relatives will not start fighting.

CAN YOU MAKE YOUR OWN WILL?

This is the biggest mistake people make. Legally, you don't need a lawyer. But it is dangerous to do it yourself. One drawback is you have no expert to testify if your will is contested. Only lawyers can give legal opinions to establish that wills are valid. Lawyers can also testify that no undue influence or pressure was put on you, which can invalidate a will.

Wills are legal documents that must comply with formal legal requirements. One small mistake can make your will invalid or delay your estate until court decisions are made. Your estate usually pays for everyone's court costs, which leaves less for beneficiaries.

Most do-it-yourself will kits contain warnings that they are not suitable for all individuals. You are responsible for correctly completing any will form. Your loved ones pay the price for incomplete or imperfectly drawn wills and can end up in court. You don't have to be rich for a battle to start.

PROFESSIONAL ADVICE REQUIRED

Lawyer-prepared wills are painless. Legal fees to prepare wills depend on your lawyer's experience and the complexity of your needs. When you average the cost over the years it can be only pennies a day for insurance to protect your loved ones. Even cheap court cases, on the other hand, cost thousands of dollars. Use your lawyer as an investment to keep your estate out of court. Have a lawyer prepare and regularly review your will.

TEST YOUR WILLPOWER

Will your will stand the test of time? You need to remember what assets can be covered by your will. Don't forget that joint owners or designated beneficiaries can also die at the same time as you, so you'll need alternative beneficiaries.

If you marry, you must make a new will. Your old one is automatically legally revoked. If you divorce, then any gift to a spouse or executor appointment is cancelled. When separating, relocating to another province or having children, you need a will update.

DID YOU PROVIDE FOR:

- your spouse, including support and property claims	**yes / no**
- any change in marital status or common-law status	**yes / no**
- special needs of children, adults and dependants	**yes / no**
- sale of your business interests	**yes / no**
- benefits for charitable causes and pets	**yes / no**
- guardians and trusts for minor children	**yes / no**
- backup executors, and back-up beneficiaries	**yes / no**

GUARDIANS

Only in a will can you name a guardian for minors and children. Make sure that when you name a guardian, you always have a backup. Your choice of guardian is always subject to final review and approval by a court. You want to consider several factors in selecting a guardian:

Age

Your elderly parents may not be able to cope with the twins. Choose someone young enough to see your children graduate.

Marital Status

Your brother may not be able to handle the twins with his own children after his divorce.

Religion

This can cause arguments so, if it is important, consider your religious preferences for guardians and any backups.

Backups

Your first choice of guardian may not be available or suitable for a court to confirm what is in the best interests of your children. Be prepared, and name a backup.

"18-KARAT" REASONS TO MAKE WILLS:

- peace of mind
- tax savings
- no delay
- provide for children
- provide for step-children
- appoint guardians
- protect dependants
- make gifts
- choose trusted executors
- reduce legal costs
- be responsible
- protect partners
- family will thank you
- its painless
- easy to change
- give to charity
- avoid family feuds
- leave a legacy

Sometimes people get hung up on small things. How should you divide up your treasured jewels, and collections? If they are valuable or family heirlooms mention them specifically in the will. You can also leave them to be divided according to you executor's discretion. A written list for distribution for your executor can be updated regularly. Such lists are morally, not legally, binding memoranda, so you may wish to list prized possessions in your will.

DEFINITIONS

Executor – also called an estate trustee in Ontario. This is your estate's legal representative, named in your will if you have one. If you have no will, "estate trustee without a will" or "administrator" refers to the same person appointed by a court.

Intestate – a dirty word meaning you died without a will. The government then writes a will for you to divide your estate. A court appoints estate trustees from your family.

Trust – if created by your will, these are called testamentary trusts. Assets are controlled or managed for the benefit of trust beneficiaries like minors or a spouse.

 Estate tip: Lawyer-prepared wills are good investments for loved ones.

CHAPTER ELEVEN

EXECUTOR IN CHARGE

"A man's dying is more the survivor's affair than his own".
– Thomas Mann

Executors, or estate trustees, answer to your beneficiaries and the courts. You need to designate an executor in your will. People often postpone making a will because they cannot decide on their executors. You may be afraid because an executor's abuse can ruin a legacy and rob beneficiaries. Choose someone honest and trustworthy to be an executor of your estate.

Remember, if you have no will, your estate's legal representative must be appointed by court. Assuming no conflict among family members, expect this process to take extra time and money. In the interval between your death and court appointment, who protects your property and loved ones? Investments can lose their value overnight without a manager.

EXECUTOR DUTIES

Your executor's authority comes from your will only if you make one. Executors must be given specific power in wills to carry out your wishes. Give them authority to handle contingencies, with professional help for your investments and business. You can protect executors from lawsuits and let them delegate administrative responsibilities.

Executors need to get tax and legal advice because they are personally liable to pay income taxes. No, it does not mean they have to pay your bills with their own money. Their liability exists only to the extent of your estate assets if taxes are not paid. To protect themselves, executors obtain estate tax clearances from Ottawa before distributing assets.

FIRST CHOICE EXECUTORS

As a rule, always pick family first. Family members usually are your beneficiaries and want to control what happens. Family will not normally charge a fee, which is taxable income of around five percent of your estate.

Who you choose as executor depends on the nature of your estate plan. Your goals may require long-term or short-term estate management. Here's the difference. Executors distribute assets usually within a year of death. Sometimes, gifts are held under a trust in your will until your children reach the age of eighteen. If this is ten years or so, you may need to consider a trust company or younger trustees.

Long-term or complex estates may need professional skills. Trust companies and professionals may be considered, or your executor can also hire your existing accountant or lawyer instead of appointing them as executors.

COMPARING CHOICES

Make sure you ask your choice of executor to consent to being named. Your first choice may not be available, so name a backup in your will. Executors may decline to act for health, personal or conflict of interest reasons. Courts can quickly appoint your alternate choice of executor if you have one named.

Here is an evaluation sheet to compare your choices.

Possible Executor	Spouse	Children	Relatives	Professional	Trust Company	Combinations
Honest Trustworthy Available						
Special Skills Required						
Must be paid a fee						
Conflicts of interest						
Trusts with long terms						
Relationships with family						

EXECUTOR REMINDERS

Name all your adult children as executors. You never know who will still be willing, able and nearby to help. Give them all the right to participate in your estate. They can always choose to renounce their role, and renouncing before acting as an executor is easy.

Once someone starts handling an estate, he or she cannot resign without court approval.

It is difficult and expensive for your beneficiaries to remove an executor for misconduct. Review your choice of executors regularly to make sure you have the best people.

Next, we will cover something your parents may have already made you: estate beneficiaries.

 Estate tip: Unless you have good reasons, family is your first choice as executors.

CHAPTER TWELVE

BENEFICIARIES GET EVERYTHING

"Love conquers all things. Let us too give in to love". – Virgil

It's easy to remember what a beneficiary is, because everyone wants to be one. Your beneficiaries are blessed at the heart of your estate. They are the reasons you plan in the first place.

In your will you can make gifts with or without conditions or you can place your gift into a trust to protect minors and spendthrift or disabled beneficiaries. Tax planning and income splitting can also be done through wills. You cannot ignore your legal obligations however, without starting a court battle after you are gone.

There are at least seven sins you do not want to commit in your will.

DON'T COMMIT THESE SEVEN SINS

1. YOU IGNORE YOUR SPOUSE.

Married spouses have rights to share in a spouse's property. Partners, same-sex or common-law, also have property and support rights which vary between provinces. You cannot ignore a spouse's legal entitlement by bypassing him or her in favour of children. Spouses who are not provided for have the right to go to court to take their legal share. All legal fees for such contests will probably be your estate's responsibility.

2. YOU DID NOT TREAT ALL CHILDREN EQUALLY.

Unless special circumstances exist, all children should share in your estate regardless of their income and position. If you don't, you will risk leaving a lifetime of pain for children who carry the burden of feeling unfairly treated. You can treat them unequally while you are alive. Paige, for example, lived with her parents and took care of them, so her parents may be justified giving her their home. However, they should tell their family while they can and deal with any problems the other children may have.

3. YOU FORGOT TO PROTECT MINOR CHILDREN.

Your will can prevent a minor's share from being paid into court and direct how a child's money will be spent and for what purposes. Create a trust to manage money for minors and name guardians. With a trust, your executor can invest and control payments to children for their educational welfare from both income and capital. Guardians will raise your children for you.

4. YOU DID NOT CONSIDER TAX CREDITS BY GIVING TO CHARITY.

After you take care of loved ones, you can be generous to charity. Remember, the charities and community organizations that mean so much to you. You can receive income tax credits by giving to charity. Stocks, RRSPs, insurance benefits, cash or antiques can all be donated. Such gifts provide a double benefit of income tax credits and reduced taxes. Advice from your favorite charities will help get maximum tax credits.

5. YOU DID NOT NAME BACKUP BENEFICIARIES.

When you plan, deal with contingencies such as your beneficiary dying. Cover yourself with backup beneficiaries to avoid unexpected results and extra expense.

6. YOU DID NOT REMEMBER THOSE WITH SPECIAL NEEDS.

Louis had been unable to keep a job and take care of his money. His parents realize he would need help with any inheritance. They set up a trust for Louis under their will allowing their trustees to hold his inheritance. All the benefits (money) from the trust go to Louis. If Louis passes away, the balance in the trust fund can go to his siblings or charity.

7. YOU DID NOT CUT SOMEONE OUT PROPERLY.

Planning to disinherit a child from your estate? Make sure you see an estate lawyer. Each province has laws that recognize children's moral and legal rights to support. Don't leave a legacy of bitterness because you didn't get invited to a child's wedding. Make sure your reasons are legitimate and that your lawyer can explain them to beneficiaries and a judge if necessary.

WHAT ABOUT SPECIFICS?

People visit my law office with detailed lists of values for each investment and asset. They want to be fair and make an equal division of their estate in their wills. If daughter, Sara gets the summer home they figure that the other children have to get equal value from other assets. The problem is that Sara's parents may not own the summer home when they die. It may also have a different value when their will is read.

It's hard to divide your estate by particular assets. Proper drafting of your will does not include naming all your bank accounts or stock holdings. Who knows if these items will still exist when you pass on?

Divide your estate into shares or percentages so that each beneficiary gets an equal share. In Sara's case, she could use her share to buy the summer home if she still wanted it.

You don't need a crystal ball to plan. Making an estate plan and a will are works in progress, and you have to keep them current to reflect your changing goals.

LET'S REVIEW

1. You need a will as an estate plan cornerstone to protect loved ones.

2. Choose executors carefully they can ruin your legacy.

3. Benefits for beneficiaries can be held in trust to protect them.

Planning also includes taking care of yourself before you die. I'll show you how to do this with powers of attorney, which should be part of every estate plan.

 Estate tip: Treat all children equally in your will unless you have good reasons not to.

PROTECT YOURSELF

USE POWERS OF ATTORNEY
AND TRUSTS.

You must appoint someone you trust to be
your attorney if you cannot make decisions.
In some cases, you may also consider trusts
for added protection for yourself or your
loved ones.

CHAPTER THIRTEEN

WHAT HAPPENS IF ...

"The time to repair the roof is when the sun is shining".
– John F. Kennedy

What if you are incapacitated by a car accident or stroke? Your spouse or children do not automatically get access to your money in case problems arise. Life goes on and your bills have to be paid. Your best protection against illness or an accident is a power of attorney for property. The alternative is to go through a court process to appoint a guardian to handle your finances. If you have not designated an attorney, thousands of dollars can be wasted through the court process.

You appoint attorneys by signing a written legal document authorizing them to act as your agent. Attorneys can do almost anything you can do, except make a will. They can act only when you are alive; executors take over after you die.

Your attorney must, by law, avoid any conflict of interest, keep financial records and have his or her work audited by the court. Family members who are also beneficiaries of your estate can be your attorneys. You can specify that your attorney is to receive a fee at rates set by government regulation.

RESTRICTIONS OR REVOCATIONS

Lisa was leaving for vacation. She wanted her daughter Donna to handle her finances while she was away. She could let Donna handle only her stock portfolio or give her, as attorney, broader powers for all financial matters. If Lisa became incapacitated, her documents must specify that Donna's powers as attorney continue or endure.

You can place conditions in the power of attorney documents to have attorneys:

- Work together if you have more than one
- Consult with accountants and business advisors if you operate a business
- Submit annual reports with tax filings to people affected by their actions

You can revoke your power of attorney if you have capacity. Revocation of a power of attorney is done in writing with two witnesses. Deliver the revocation to your attorney and financial institutions if necessary and destroy any existing copies of the power of attorney.

CAUTION

Documents that contain no restrictions are effective once you sign and have them witnessed. Ask your attorney to consent first and always name a backup. You don't need to give a copy to your attorney in advance but advise him or her where your documents are stored.

Be realistic about possible attorney abuse, mismanagement and loss of assets. You can protect yourself by naming more than one attorney so they work together. If you are required to act as someone's attorney, make sure you get proper legal advice on your duties and responsibilities.

QUALITIES YOUR ATTORNEYS NEED

– honesty
– trustworthiness
– ability to be close at hand
– available to consult with financial advisors

POSSIBLE CHOICES FOR ATTORNEY

– same persons as executors or estate beneficiaries
– spouse or family member over 18 in the same city or province
– combination of family member and professional advisor
– people with no conflict of interest

Protect yourself before you become incapacitated and sign a power of attorney for your finances.

You also have to consider one other type of power of attorney: one for health care decisions. We will look at this, living wills and medical directives in the next chapter.

DEFINITIONS

Attorney – an agent you name by signing a written legal document called power of attorney. Two qualified witnesses are required. You usually have one attorney for health and one for finances.

Personal care attorney – a person you designate by signing a power of attorney to make health and personal care decisions when you cannot.

Attorney for property – handles financial decisions specified in the power of attorney documents.

CHAPTER FOURTEEN

PULLING THE PLUG

"...for a dying person it is a duty and a necessity to give serious attention to himself". - Carl Jung

Elaine wants to communicate her final health care wishes in advance, to settle her fears. Her favorite television talk show calls it "pulling the plug." Powers of attorney for health decisions allow her to designate an attorney who communicates her personal care wishes. Her attorney can act only if Elaine is incapable of making her own decisions for health care, safety, hygiene, clothing and medical treatment.

Your health care providers could assess you as unable to understand the consequences of health decisions. Incapacity can occur because of a stroke, car accident or disease at any age. Your care provider turns to your attorney for decisions. You cannot be bypassed by your attorney for personal care unless you are incapacitated.

Attorneys for personal care are designated to communicate your wishes in the event that you cannot. Powers of attorney for personal care are written legal documents. You name a person or people to make or communicate your wishes if you cannot. These people by law must be guided by instructions you may leave in writing, or orally. In the absence of both, they normally must consider decisions based on your values.

QUALITIES FOR A PERSONAL CARE ATTORNEY

1. ability to communicate your wishes

2. ability to meet with your care professionals

3. trusted close friend or family member

4. could be same person as executor or financial attorney

Living wills are actually misnomers. They don't deal with assets after one's death, but usually medical care issues before a person dies. You can attach living wills or instructions to your power of attorney for personal care document for extra guidance and comfort.

It's better to have a power of attorney as your main document authorizing an agent to make decisions. Your instructions in medical directives may quickly become irrelevant or out of date. Living wills with your instructions in the pull-the-plug scenarios may have little relevance for your care.

Here is a quick list of comparisons of the different documents we have talked about.

Medical directive or living will

- no agent or attorney is named to deal with property
- addressed to care providers
- may not have valid witnesses
- may bind your attorney as it reflects your wishes
- validity may be questioned

Power of attorney for personal care

- designates person for health care issues
- must be written with legal requirements for witnesses
- can be revoked
- can provide direction and guidance for choices
- valid only once you no longer can make decisions yourself

Power of attorney for property

- designates person for financial decisions and property
- should specify and authorize agent in the event of incapacity
- restrictions can be put into document
- can be revoked
- valid once signed

Attorneys for personal care are designated to communicate your wishes in the event that you cannot. In some cases, you can protect yourself by using a trust. I'll explain this in the next chapter.

 Estate tip: Everyone's estate toolbox should contain powers of attorney for personal care.

CHAPTER FIFTEEN

SPEAKING OF TRUSTS

"Put not your trust in money, but your money in trust."
- Oliver Wendell Holmes

Maria was disabled after recently arriving in Canada. Kelly and her co-workers raised money to pay for her medical care. Kelly was named trustee to handle the money collected which she held "in trust" for Maria's care. This is an example of a trust with Kelly acting as trustee of the trust fund for Maria's benefit.

Think of trusts as involving three people in a legal relationship to manage assets for the benefit of the beneficiaries.

HOW TRUSTS ARE CREATED

Here's how a trust can be set up.

1. You transfer assets to your trustee under a trust agreement. This can be done when you are alive or after your death in your will.

2. Trustees, whom you name, manage the trust property under the terms set out in your trust documents.

3. Beneficiaries are named in the trust document, and they receive benefits from the assets held in trust. If the trust assets produce income, you can specify if trustees can spend just income or capital of the trust as well.

You can pay a lawyer while you're alive to create a trust, which would be called a living trust. Living trusts can be used for holding special assets like company shares or a vacation property. You would consider these tools for their tax planning advantages and the protection of beneficiaries.

Testamentary trusts are the most common trusts and are easily created by your will. Everyone who has minor children or beneficiaries with special needs or spendthrift habits needs to include a trust in their will. Trustees, who can also be executors under your will, are legally obligated to manage assets for the benefit of the third parties.

TRUST ADVANTAGES

Without a trust, a minor child's inheritance must be paid into court and held until he or she is 18. Creating a trust for minors in your will allows you to:

- have the investment portfolio professionally managed by trustees
- separate legal ownership of the trust assets from benefits of ownership
- ensure that someone you consider reliable will be responsible for your children's needs

Trusts can allow trustees to spend capital or income, and you can specify the spending terms and conditions for your children's benefit.

Trustees must file tax returns to report trust income. Living trusts are taxed at the highest flat rate, which is the top combined federal and provincial rate.

Testamentary trusts, on the other hand, are taxed at graduated or variable individual rates, which can be lower than the highest rates. Trusts created by your will allow you to split income with trust beneficiaries who could, for example, be your grandchildren or a spouse.

TRUSTS AND WILLS

The terms of a living trust are not public information. After your death, trustees could transfer assets directly to your beneficiaries named in the trust. These beneficiaries could be the same as those under your will.

Even after you get professional advice to prepare a living trust, you still need a will. Wills appoint a legal representative for your estate and are much less expensive to prepare than living trusts.

No probate taxes are paid when you transfer assets into the trust, and the terms and conditions of the trust would be kept private. It may be very difficult to successfully challenge the trust. This prevents your estate goals from being set aside by a legal contest over your will.

ALTER EGO AND JOINT PARTNER TRUSTS

Are you 65 or older and in the top tax bracket? Then you may benefit from alter ego or joint spousal trusts since 1999. You can use these living trusts to avoid probate fees, publicity and power of attorney abuses. Here's how: you transfer assets tax-free to special qualifying trusts you create while alive. Normally, when you transfer assets into trusts you trigger capital gains. But tax law changes now allow you to defer the deemed disposition rules until you or your spouse die.

You will need a lawyer to prepare written trust documents to set up the trust. These trusts can help you avoid having a contest over your capacity if you are ill or elderly. Trustees handle matters that attorneys may not be able to deal with because of restrictions on an attorney's legal authority. You may be a trustee while you are competent, but legally, only you or a spouse may be entitled to income or capital from the trust while you are alive.

You can designate who beneficiaries of the trust will be after the last of you and your partner pass away. This bypasses probate, and the larger the estate the larger the probate savings. Privacy may be important as the trust does not get probated or filed with a court. Wills, remember are public documents and can be contested especially when relatives are disenchanted with their share.

Life insurance is confusing to many people, so we'll explore that in the next section.

 Estate tip: Trusts give you power to control assets for the benefit of others.

CONSIDER EXTRAS

INSURANCE, BUSINESS AND EXECUTOR'S WORK.

Life insurance can solve your estate's cash flow problems and protect business assets you pass on to loved ones. Learn what's involved in "settling an estate" in three easy steps.

CHAPTER SIXTEEN

TAX-FREE LIFE INSURANCE

"If a man doesn't believe in life insurance, let him die without it. That will teach him a lesson." - Will Rogers

Carl never got life insurance. He lost his life in a freak construction accident. Sue-Anne, his wife and mother of their twins, now faces many problems. She no longer has her husband's income to cover mortgage payments, and is forced to sell her family's home. Like many people, Carl did not know how to buy insurance. He should have found an insurance professional to help protect his loved ones.

WHY BUY LIFE INSURANCE?

Here are some reasons to buy life insurance:

* **Replace income.** Your family may lose the benefit of your income. How will they cover major expenses, children's education and mortgage payments?

* **Pay your debts.** Preview your estate to calculate cash required to pay your expenses. Funeral, income tax, probate costs and debts add up.

* **Create an estate.** If you are not wealthy, insurance creates substantial assets for your loved ones to inherit. Keep in mind that life insurance proceeds are tax-free benefits.

* **Business reasons.** Insurance can cover business loans, partnership or shareholders agreements and fund a buyout from an estate.

Life insurance policies through employment or separate coverage can guarantee gifts for minors and dependants from a prior marriage. Insurance payable to children (use a trust if they are minors) will guarantee tax-free, creditor-proof benefits for loved ones.

What if you want your children to inherit assets with tax liabilities like your business or rental property? Watch out for the tax bill, or they may have to sell the very asset you left them to pay taxes. Life insurance can cover the debts to Ottawa and leave your gifts intact.

WHAT INSURANCE TO BUY?

Insurance comes in two basic categories, term and permanent life, which covers your "whole life." Your insurance representative will explain the many variations available with each type of plan. Talk to a few agents or develop a relationship with a broker whom you trust. Find one interested in selling you appropriate amounts and types of insurance for your needs. Let's look at both kinds of life insurance.

TERM INSURANCE

Think of it as insurance for a period of time with a variety of options. Term insurance is often the best and only affordable way for a young family to be adequately insured. You can use term insurance to insure at relatively low cost but understand that it:

1. Protects only for a specified term of years
2. Premiums increase based on your age and health.
3. Has no cash or investment value when you stop paying

PERMANENT INSURANCE

Permanent insurance comes in whole life, universal and variable life. It can be used as a more advanced estate and tax planning tool. Essentially, permanent insurance:

1. Provides guaranteed lifetime coverage regardless of health or age
2. Is more expensive than term but is guaranteed to death
3. Has some cash value if you need to cancel it.

Consider Roberto. He is a 35-year-old non-smoking male. He can be insured with a million-dollar death benefit with a 20-year term policy for about $120 per month. At age 55, Roberto may not need term life insurance. He could donate his policy to charity and use the tax credits to reduce his estate's tax bill. On the other hand, by that age he may have a business agreement to buy or sell his company's shares. Perhaps he needs cash to pay the capital gains tax on recreational property he wants to keep in the family. For these needs, a permanent policy would be more appropriate.

You can use insurance to prepare for the unexpected and with professional help, it can be used to develop tax and estate strategies. Set your goals and get an insurance assessment, then review your options and coverage costs. Younger families with dependants need to fund future living costs for premature deaths of a financial provider.

DEFINITIONS

Permanent Insurance - usually has fixed death benifits, level premium payment and a cash value if cancelled before you die. Term insurance, on the other hand, provides coverage for a term of years.

Universal Life – has flexible premiums and pay-out values and you can adjust amounts of coverage and make some withdrawals.

Variable Insurance – has two elements and is referred to as a segregated fund contract. Usually premiums are fixed and benefits vary with performance of your assets in separate or segregated funds. This fund fluctuates like equity in mutual funds.

If you want to start a business, or have a family member in a business, you'll want to review the next chapter.

Estate tip: Define your protection needs and get independent insurance advice.

CHAPTER SEVENTEEN

BUSINESS BUYOUTS

"Seest thou a man diligent in his business, he shall stand before kings." - Proverbs

What do you do if you own a business? How you own your business makes a difference when you plan. You need to understand that businesses can be divided into three major categories, and each affects how you plan.

Many versions or variations exist in each category such as limited partnerships, joint ventures, private or public corporations. Here's a quick overview.

1. SOLE PROPRIETORSHIPS

In this arrangement, you are the only owner and personally responsible for the business debts. You receive all income, which is reported on your personal income tax return. This is an inexpensive way to carry on business. In Harold's Hardware and Software, if Harold dies owning this business, it will be treated as a will asset. His estate will have to satisfy all his trade creditors. Sounds risky, because your creditors' claims can wipe out your estate. Sole proprietors have that kind of unlimited liability.

2. PARTNERSHIPS

If Harold and Maude run the business for profit it may be a partnership. Partners report profit and losses personally so this can affect either partner's estate. Partnerships require a written agreement, for the surviving partner to buy out the deceased's interest. Without this agreement, the partnership ceases business operations when the partner dies.

3. CORPORATIONS

Corporations are separate legal entities distinct from their shareholders and they file their own tax returns to pay tax on reported income. Corporations can credit-proof your estate by shielding personal assets for the benefit of loved ones.

BUSINESS PLANNING

As a sole proprietor, you must have a will to allow executors to operate the business after you die. Partners and shareholders need buy/sell agreements to deal with the death of a business owner. Under the buy/sell agreement, the surviving shareholder or partner is committed to purchase the deceased's business interests. This is an important estate planning tool as in most businesses there are few if any realistic opportunities to find alternative buyers.

INCORPORATING YOUR BUSINESS

Are you in business and not incorporated? Your personal assets can be at risk, as creditors and customers can sue and collect from you as well as from business assets. Incorporation can limit this liability to the extent of the corporation's assets. Having a corporation can also make a tax difference when someone buys your business.

Some corporations qualify as small business corporations resulting in a low rate of tax. Another tax benefit exists if your corporation is an active business operating in Canada. A $500,000 capital gains deduction may be available on the sale of qualifying corporate shares. This can produce sizable tax savings if you meet certain requirements, so get professional help to take advantage of the small business deduction.

BUSINESS BUY/SELL

What if you die while owning a partnership interest or shares in a private corporation? These assets, unless jointly owned, will be covered by your will. You need buy/sell agreements to have a corporation or partner buy or redeem your interests. Life insurance proceeds can be used to fund the purchase price.

If you are a business owner, ask this important question: Where is the money going to come from to buy out your interest? Different events can trigger a buyout, so consider disability, retirement, succession planning and death in your agreement.

Normally, life insurance covers the buyout costs, but not in all cases. Written buy/sell agreements protect your heirs by making sure that they can realize your business equity.

Let's give you a context for the estate planning you have learned so far as we look at the steps you take to settle an estate. You'll be able to see things through the eyes of your executor.

Estate tip: Incorporate to qualify for estate protection and small business advantages.

CHAPTER EIGHTEEN

SETTLE YOUR ESTATE

"It's a funny old world. A man is lucky if he gets out of it alive."
– Walter de Leon and Paul M. Jones

Do you know what to do when somebody dies? Here's what you need to know if you have been asked to be an executor. This will help you understand how to select your own executor.

Remember, executors do not have to perform legal work. They must be trustworthy, financially responsible and hire the right professionals to guide them. Here is an outline of an executor's duties in three steps:

Step 1. Protect estate property by making sure it is secure and insured
Step 2. Probate the will if necessary to sell or transfer assets
Step 3. Pay bills and distribute the estate to beneficiaries

STEP 1 PROTECT ASSETS

If you are an executor or trustee, your first step is to see a lawyer. Make sure the will you have is valid and is really the last one signed. If not, you could be liable to the real beneficiaries. Secure assets by making sure insurance is in place for cars, homes and valuables. Lawyers will educate you about executor duties and how you can protect yourself from liability.

You can help your executor by making lists of valuables, debts and documents. Even your own spouse will not know everything about your assets and liabilities. Look at the documents we referred to in Chapter 2 so someone can have ready access to insurance, lists of assets and debts for quick updating.

Lawyers need a list of debts, assets and details are always helpful to make sure nothing is missed. Your executor can save time by using your list of assets and liabilities in case you and your partner pass away together. You don't have to specify what suit you want to be decked out in, but you can identify your preferences for the type of funeral services. Remember your beneficiaries may appreciate receiving those items that had sentimental or personal significance for them.

Executors have a duty to account for all financial dealings if necessary before a court, and therefore need legal advice at the outset to protect themselves. Problems often arise that could easily have been prevented with proper advice.

A box of books donated to a charity may contain valuable first editions. How does an executor defend a claim for executor's negligence? Record keeping should start at the onset and continue until beneficiaries or a judge approves all transactions. In some cases, executors may need to keep records of time they spend to justify their claims for compensation.

STEP 2 PROBATE WILLS

Executors hire lawyers to obtain probate so the court can certify the persons entitled under a last will. Your assets are valued to calculate probate taxes, and getting up to date appraisals of property, investments and any business will take some time. If you have a will, an executor's authority to act on your estate's behalf comes from it, which can allow him or her to act immediately. If you have no will, the court must appoint an estate trustee which is time consuming and expensive.

Probate proves to third parties that a court has validated your will. Until probate is obtained, executors need legal advice to manage estate assets. Investment decisions may need to be made after meeting initially with a planner or tax advisors. Executors are liable to your beneficiaries and creditors, so your will should protect them from honest mistakes and falling markets. Therefore, in your will you should provide your executor with discretion and specific powers to sell, set terms, settle claims and set prices.

STEP 3 PAY EVERYONE

Executors wait until all your debts, including income tax, are settled and they receive an estate clearance certificate from Ottawa. In some cases, executors will want also to advertise for creditors. This protects the executor from personal exposure for income tax and other liabilities. Releases are usually signed once beneficiaries approve the distribution and executor compensation.

Here is a summary of tips for executors.

MORE THAN A DOZEN TIPS FOR EXECUTORS

STEP ONE: PROTECT ASSETS

1. Review the will and contact a lawyer.
2. Confirm the funeral arrangements.
3. Take steps to secure the estate property.
4. Notify the next of kin and beneficiaries.
5. Guarantee insurance coverage on valuables.
6. Preserve any business or investments.

STEP TWO: PROBATE WILLS

7. Prepare an inventory of assets and liabilities.
8. Hire a lawyer to probate the will.
9. Settle all legal issues.
10. Sell assets to pay bills.

STEP THREE: PAY EVERYONE

11. Pay all liabilities and get income tax clearance certificate.
12. Account to the beneficiaries.
13. Have your executor's compensation approved.
14. Get a release signed from all beneficiaries.
15. Distribute the estate assets.

CAN WILLS BE CHALLENGED?

In some cases, wills are challenged and a court is asked to declare a will invalid. Wills can be declared invalid because of fraud, duress and undue influence. The person making the allegations must prove them in court. This is another benefit of having a lawyer-prepared will. They are harder to attack because lawyers keep notes and can testify in court. Now you have another reason not to wait until you go to the hospital to make your will.

Before rushing to carry out a deceased's wishes, call the lawyer who prepared the will. Make sure there are no codicils or questions about validity. Remember, handwritten holographic wills, written entirely in the deceased's own handwriting, can be valid wills in some provinces.

 Estate tip: Protect, probate and pay are an executor's three responsibilities.

REVIEW CHANGES

REVISE AND RECORD

Let us look at the three R's in estate planning:
review, revise and record.

CHAPTER NINETEEN

REVIEW FOR CHANGES

"There is nothing permanent except change". – Heracleitus

Your will must reflect the changes in your own life circumstances. One way you can make changes is in a codicil, which is an inexpensive document that covers minor legal changes to your will.

Codicils are written amendments to existing wills and require compliance with the usual legal requirements for a valid will. You must sign in front of two witnesses who are not beneficiaries or spouses of beneficiaries. You should not risk trying to make amendments to your will by yourself.

Codicils are best used for minor changes such as replacing an executor or the cash amount of a gift to grandchildren. Any subsequent additional changes would normally be included in a revised will to simplify the probate process.

CHANGING IS NOT ALTERING

Remember, that changing your will is not the same as making a change "on" your will. Altering your daughter's last name on your will by scratching it out may make the will invalid if not properly witnessed and executed.

If you write on or alter your original will, you can be in trouble. Courts ignore changes on your wills unless signed in front of two witnesses. Some alterations require court rulings to ensure that you were not trying to revoke or cancel your will.

TOP TEN REASONS TO CHANGE YOUR WILL

1. you divorce, separate or cohabit with a new partner
2. children are born or you need new guardians
3. you now have grandchildren or stepchildren
4. a person named in your will becomes ill, disabled or dies
5. you need to change executors, beneficiaries, or charities
6. your assets have increased and you want more tax planning
7. you start a business
8. you move to another province or country
9. you acquire major assets in another province or country
10. your children become adults

HOW TO CANCEL WILLS

This is called revoking your will by tearing, burning or destroying the original. Each time you make a will, you usually include these words "I hereby revoke all previous wills or codicils." Just by making a new will, you can revoke all prior wills. Your will is also revoked whenever you marry. One exception to this is a will made in contemplation of your marriage, after your engagement and before the honeymoon.

STORING ORIGINAL DOCUMENTS

Help people locate your original documents with a document inventory as described in the appendix of this book. Only the original will, not the copies, will be valid. If no one can find your original will, you will end up dying without one. Spare everyone the trouble of going crazy looking for your will. Tell your executors where to expect to find your documents.

Include your inventory of assets and debts with the original will, and while you are at it specify your burial preferences. You do not have to go into great detail. Funeral arrangements unless prearranged and prepaid are not legally binding on your executor. The same applies to your distribution list for knick-knacks. Such lists have moral weight but are not legally binding on beneficiaries. If valuable or critical for your peace of mind, include items like your antique Rolls-Royce in your will.

Some lawyers and trust companies provide free storage if they prepare your will. Make sure storage is fireproof. Bank safe deposit boxes offer protection from fire, flood and risk of destruction.

LAWYERS AND CHANGES

Frequently, lawyers who may have prepared your will retire or die. If a lawyer keeps your original will, you may have to locate his or her successor. Law Society records can be used to find your will. Usually your lawyer will be able to provide you with the documents needed to file for probate of your will.

If your will was prepared long ago your witnesses may not be alive, and you may be better off to sign an update. Chances are, you would benefit from a review and revision. You do not have to return to your original lawyer to make changes to your will.

Are you becoming a bride or a groom? Your entire estate plan needs updating. You can learn all about these marital changes in the next chapter.

DEFINITIONS

Revocation – cancels your will by destruction or when you make a new one.

Codicils – legal documents used for minor changes or amendments to your will

Marriage Contracts – lawyer-prepared agreements; also called prenups. You sign before or during marriage to deal with family and estate plan issues. Each spouse needs his or her own lawyer.

 Estate tip: Prepare a record of where your original estate planning documents are stored.

CHAPTER TWENTY

MARRIED, SEPARATED OR DIVORCED?

"The fellow who courts trouble often marries her". – Old Postcard

Getting married, separated or divorced, can however, collapse your estate plan. You need to understand and use this information to set new goals for your estate plan. Marriage creates new planning priorities, which, especially in a second marriage, will usually require expert advice.

MARRIAGE CONTRACT MERRY-GO-ROUND

Doctor Dan married for the second time, but he wants his estate to go to his adult children from his first marriage. His new spouse's legal rights can affect his estate plan, and he must not ignore her entitlement. He needs to consider a marriage contract to secure his assets for his children.

Prenuptial domestic agreements or marriage contracts are often considered deal breakers. Everyone worries how his or her partner will react when the topic is mentioned. Here are pointers on why you may need a prenup:

- Anyone with assets, dependants and doubts going into a marriage should get his or her own legal advice.

- Marriage contracts require each person to have separate lawyers to ensure that the contract will not be thrown out of court.

- Contracts are negotiated, and no ultimatums or terms of surrender should be made.

- Be prepared to make full disclosure of all your assets and debts. In some cases, proper valuations or appraisals may be requested.

- If you want a contract, get it signed before the big day. You need a couple of months for drafting and negotiating to avoid pressure that can ruin a wedding.

CHECKLIST FOR THE BRIDE AND GROOM

This is not a wedding but a legal checklist for everyone planning to get married, for the first or second time.

1. REVIEW ASSETS WITH BENEFICIARY DESIGNATIONS.
Check RRSPs, RIFs, life insurance and pension benefits. Make sure your medical, drug and benefits correctly include your spouse.

2. CONSIDER A MARRIAGE CONTRACT.
If appropriate, you can protect family or business assets and growth potential of property by agreeing to keep assets separate from division in case of a breakup.

3. UPDATE YOUR WILL.
Marriage automatically revokes your will so make a new will in contemplation of marriage. Your new spouse's share can be conditional on the marriage proceeding. Don't forget to cover events like the marriage not going ahead.

4. NAME THE RIGHT PERSON.
Change your executors, attorneys, and beneficiaries once you divorce, remarry or separate.

SEPARATED OR DIVORCED?

Remember, marriage revokes your will but divorce terminates any gift or appointment as executor to your divorced spouse. If divorced, your will would be read as if your former spouse had not inherited anything from your estate.

CAN YOU DISINHERIT A SEPARATED SPOUSE FROM YOUR ESTATE?

Family property and support laws give your spouse an interest in your estate so you cannot cut him or her out. This means that you cannot defeat a separated spouse's entitlement to your estate by not mentioning him or her in your will. You can, however, make sure that he or she does not get your entire estate or more than is necessary with careful planning.

What about leaving everything in trust to your spouse and then when he or she dies it can be passed on to your children? If you wish to create a life estate for a partner, don't ever try to do it alone. You need to perform sophisticated calculations and projections to deal with tax, trust and family law issues. Get help from a lawyer well versed in all these areas.

Frequently, creating a trust for a surviving spouse can be more of a burden than a blessing. Spouses who receive income from a trust may find that they need more than you anticipated giving from your estate. They may be forced to deal with the desires of children, perhaps from a first marriage. This can mean retaining lawyers and perhaps going to court.

Every time you marry separate and divorce or move from another jurisdiction, review your estate plan to make sure your real loved ones and your legal obligations are covered.

 Estate tip: Changes in marital status requires changes to your estate plan.

CHAPTER TWENTY-ONE

WRAP-UP

"The heart has its reasons, which reason does not know."
– Blaise Pascal

Congratulations! You now have learned the essentials to successful estate planning. *Estate to the Heart* should help you and your family avoid a forced estate sale. Your loved ones will not waste your estate on unnecessary taxes, delays and legal expenses. You can be happy with peace of mind, worry-free that family, friends and charities have been looked after.

You can start to construct an action plan with your professional advisors. Take steps now before one of life's big surprises comes along to create a crisis. Get the cornerstones, up to-date wills and powers of attorney in place to feel that a big load has been lifted. But you cannot stop there, since estate planning, taking care of loved ones, is a lifelong process.

PROTECT YOUR LOVED ONES

You will have to make more decisions as you deal with life's different challenges. When you are single with few assets, planning is not complicated. You may start a business and need powers of attorney to protect yourself. As you marry and have children, wills, insurance, trust accounts and guardianship issues become important. As you get older you may find that you want your parents, children and friends to read this book.

TIPS TO SUCCESS

"Why should I worry about estate planning?" Consider planning as an act of love and not a chore that you keep postponing. Do it together with your partner on Valentine's day, your anniversary or your birtday. Remember these seven essentials whenever major changes occur:

1. TAKE ACTION. Think of your estate as another word for your loved ones. Effective estate plans give you the power to reach your goals to benefit those closest to you. Professional advice helps you reach your goals with less pain and trouble.

2. IDENTIFY ASSETS. You can distribute property in three ways. Jointly owned assets with rights of survivorship pass automatically on your death. Assets with designated beneficiaries can also bypass probate. Contingencies like beneficiaries or joint owners dying first, and any other assets, are covered by your will.

3. PREVIEW DEBTS. Avoid surprises by first factoring probate and income taxes into calculations of what will be in your estate. What will you have left over if ten percent of your estate covers estate expenses before taxes?

4. MAKE WILLS. Most people think estate planning is just making a will, but you need more than a will to cover all the bases. Planning means that you keep all documents current with your goals and beneficiaries' needs.

5. PROTECT YOURSELF. You need powers of attorney to insure that the government does not step in to make decisions for you. You really can protect yourself, your estate and personal dignity with these documents.

6. CONSIDER EXTRAS. You need to know that estate administration includes business issues and life insurance's tax-free advantages. Reviewing an executor's duties will give you a new prospective on planning.

7. REVIEW CHANGES. You must record and update inventories of assets, debts and documents so others will find them. If no one can find your will, you will have died without one.

Now you understand the fundamentals and can get professional help to avoid nightmares for your heirs. You will feel better knowing you have the right person for each job as executor, attorney and advisor.

NOT THE DIRTY DOZEN

ESTATE PLANNING CHECKLIST

Make sure your good intentions become a reality. Create and maintain a document inventory of estate planning tools, assets and debts. Make a note if you need to talk to someone about being a guardian or executor.

Some of these documents may not apply, so mark them not applicable (N/A).

1. Asset and document inventory – completed	**yes**	**no**
2. Estate goal outline – completed	**yes**	**no**
3. Will/partner's will – completed	**yes**	**no**
4. Financial powers of attorney - completed	**yes**	**no**
5. Personal care powers of attorney - completed	**yes**	**no**
6. Marriage, cohabitation agreement - completed	**yes**	**no**
7. Trusts for special needs or minors – completed	**yes**	**no**
8. Guardianship for minor children – completed	**yes**	**no**
9. Business buy/sell agreement - completed	**yes**	**no**
10. Insurance inventory - completed	**yes**	**no**
11. Estate preview to minimize taxes completed	**yes**	**no**
12. Record estate plan review – completed	**yes**	**no**

Now that you have read this book you will understand the essentials of estate planning. Use your knowledge to protect your loved ones with more than good intentions. Make an action plan and get professional advice. Take advantage of the time you have to guard those closest to your heart. Put your heart into estate planning for your loved ones' sake.

 Estate tip: When you prepare for the future, look on the bright side.

ESTATE TO THE HEART TOOLS

"THANK YOU" FILE

You can photocopy your documents and put them into a folder marked: "Thank You" That is what everyone will do when they find it.

ASSET INVENTORY

Help your loved ones manage a difficult situation if something happens to you. Lists can help you communicate where your assets can be found. Divide your assets into three categories that make up your estate pie: joint assets, designated assets and will assets.

ESTATE TO THE HEART

Here are some of the things you should record here or on a computer to make it easy to update.

ESTATE ASSET INVENTORY

Asset	Joint Asset	Designated Asset	Will Asset
1. Personal property (cars, boats, art)			
2. Life insurance			
3. Private and government pensions			
4. RRIFs, RRSPs and annuities			
5. Home or real estate			
6. Bonds, stocks, and mutual funds			
7. Bank accounts and certificates			
8. Business Interests			

Record where these assets can be located on your list of assets.

- Location of safety deposit box
- List of contents
- Location of key and necessary documents for access

Now do the same for your debts.

DEBTS

Here is where you list your liabilities or photocopy particulars for:

1. Bank loans
2. Personal loans
3. Credit cards
4. Mortgage/other loans

INSURANCE LIST

	Agent/Broker	Details
a) Life insurance:		
b) Home insurance:		
c) Car insurance:		
d) Business insurance:		

PROFESSIONAL ADVISERS

1. NAME OF MY ESTATE LAWYER: _____

   FIRM: _____

   ADDRESS: _____

   TELEPHONE: _____

2. NAME OF MY ACCOUNTANT: _____

   FIRM: _____

   ADDRESS: _____

   TELEPHONE: _____

3. NAME OF MY FINANCIAL ADVISER: _____

   FIRM: _____

   ADDRESS: _____

   TELEPHONE: _____

4. NAME OF MY LIFE INSURANCE AGENT: _____

    FIRM: _____

    ADDRESS: _____

    TELEPHONE: _____

5. NAME OF MY BUSINESS LAWYER: _____

    FIRM: _____

    ADDRESS: _____

    TELEPHONE: _____

6. NAME OF MY INVESTMENT/STOCK BROKER: _____

    FIRM: _____

    ADDRESS: _____

    TELEPHONE: _____

DOCUMENT INVENTORY

It will be useful for your survivors to know the whereabouts of relevant documents. List the particulars for professionals who handle your affairs.

WILLS

DATE OF WILL AND CODICILS: _____

ORIGINAL STORED AT: _____

EXECUTOR: _____

ADDRESS: _____

TELEPHONE: _____

DATE OF SPOUSE'S WILL AND CODICILS: _____

ORIGINAL STORED AT: _____

EXECUTOR: _____

POWERS OF ATTORNEY FOR PROPERTY

DATE OF DOCUMENT: _____

ORIGINAL STORED AT: _____

NAME OF ATTORNEY: _____

ADDRESS: _____

TELEPHONE: _____

DATE OF SPOUSE'S ORIGINAL: _____

ORIGINAL STORED AT: _____

ATTORNEY: _____

ADDRESS: _____

TELEPHONE: _____

POWERS OF ATTORNEY FOR PERSONAL CARE

DATE OF DOCUMENT: _____

ORIGINAL STORED AT: _____

NAME OF ATTORNEY: _____

ADDRESS: _____

TELEPHONE: _____

DATE OF SPOUSE'S ORIGINAL: _____

ORIGINAL STORED AT: _____

NAME OF ATTORNEY: _____

ADDRESS: _____

TELEPHONE: _____

IMPORTANT DOCUMENTS

1. Birth Certificate

2. Marriage Certificate

3. Citizenship and government documents

4. Location of other documents including separation agreements, divorce judgements and marriage contacts.

5. Memo of distribution of personal assets

6. Deeds/titles to property

7. Passwords with PIN numbers

FUNERAL ARRANGEMENTS

I WOULD LIKE TO BE BURIED _____ OR CREMATED _____.

I WOULD LIKE TO USE THIS FUNERAL HOME:

NAME: _____

ADDRESS: _____

TELEPHONE: _____

CONTACT: _____

I HAVE THE FOLLOWING ARRANGEMENTS ALREADY IN PLACE.

LOCATION OF PRE-ARRANGEMENT CONTRACT:

_____

_____

RELIGIOUS SERVICES

CLERGYMEN: _____

MUSIC: _____

FLOWER: _____

MEMORIALS: _____

OTHER REQUESTS: _____

_____

CEMETERY ARRANGEMENTS

NAME OF CEMETERY: _____

ADDRESS: _____

TELEPHONE: _____

LOCATION OF DEED: _____

PLOT IN NAME OF: _____

SECTION: _____ PLOT NUMBER: _____

WILL PLANNING NOTES

YOUR PERSONAL INFORMATION

_____

FULL NAME

_____

MARITAL STATUS

_____

ADDRESS

_____

HOME PHONE NUMBER

_____

BUSINESS NUMBER

_____

EMAIL ADDRESS

_____

OCCUPATION

_____

EMPLOYED BY OR RETIRED FROM

_____

RELIGIOUS AFFILIATION

_____

FATHER'S NAME AND MOTHER'S MAIDEN NAME

CITIZENSHIP

PLACE AND DATE OF BIRTH

PLACE AND DATE OF MARRIAGE

DO YOU HAVE A MARRIAGE CONTRACT?

HAVE YOU BEEN MARRIED BEFORE?

PLACE AND DATE OF DIVORCE

DO YOU HAVE A SEPARATION AGREEMENT?

DO YOU HAVE CHILDREN FROM A PREVIOUS RELATIONSHIP?

DETAILS OF ANY SUPPORT OBLIGATIONS

PLACE AND DATE OF DIVORCE

YOUR SPOUSE'S INFORMATION

FULL NAME

MARITAL STATUS

ADDRESS

HOME PHONE NUMBER

BUSINESS NUMBER

EMAIL ADDRESS

OCCUPATION

EMPLOYED BY OR RETIRED FROM

RELIGIOUS AFFILIATION

FATHER'S NAME AND MOTHER'S MAIDEN NAME

CITIZENSHIP

PLACE AND DATE OF BIRTH

PLACE AND DATE OF MARRIAGE

DO YOU HAVE A MARRIAGE CONTRACT?

HAVE YOU BEEN MARRIED BEFORE?

PLACE AND DATE OF DIVORCE

DO YOU HAVE A SEPARATION AGREEMENT?

DO YOU HAVE CHILDREN FROM A PREVIOUS RELATIONSHIP?

DETAILS OF ANY SUPPORT OBLIGATIONS

PLACE AND DATE OF DIVORCE

INFORMATION ON CHILDREN

1. FULL NAME

ADDRESS

DATE OF BIRTH

MARITAL STATUS

OCCUPATION

SPOUSE'S OCCUPATION

2. FULL NAME

ADDRESS

DATE OF BIRTH

MARITAL STATUS

OCCUPATION

SPOUSE'S OCCUPATION

3. FULL NAME

ADDRESS

DATE OF BIRTH

MARITAL STATUS

4. FULL NAME

ADDRESS

DATE OF BIRTH

MARITAL STATUS

OTHER BENEFICIARIES TO CONSIDER

_____

FULL NAME

_____

ADDRESS

_____

DATE OF BIRTH

_____

RELATIONSHIP TO YOU

OTHER BENEFICIARIES TO CONSIDER

_____

FULL NAME

_____

ADDRESS

_____

DATE OF BIRTH

_____

RELATIONSHIP TO YOU

CHARITIES, CHURCHES, CAUSES: _____

_____

_____

THE RIGHT PERSON FOR EVERY JOB LIST

1. Name of possible executor: _____

   Relationship: _____

   Address: _____

   Telephone: _____

2. Name of possible backup executor: _____

   Relationship: _____

   Address: _____

   Telephone: _____

3. Name of guardian for minor children: _____

   Relationship: _____

   Address: _____

   Telephone: _____

4. Name of backup guardian for minor children:

   _____

   Relationship: _____

   Address: _____

   Telephone: _____

GLOSSARY

ATTORNEY - an agent you name by signing written legal documents called a power of attorney. Two qualified witnesses are required.

ATTORNEY FOR PERSONAL CARE - a person you designate by signing a power of attorney to make health care decisions when you can't.

ATTORNEY FOR PROPERTY - handles only financial and property decisions as specified in the power of attorney document you sign.

CAPITAL GAINS - capital property has a fair market value (FMV) at your death. The difference between FMV and asset cost may be a gain. A portion of this gain is included on your tax return as income.

CODICILS - legal documents used to revise or amend your will.

DEEMED DISPOSITION - at death you are deemed to have received fair market value (FMV) for all capital property. It's deemed sold even if your estate gets no actual sale proceeds, only a tax liability. Capital property includes real estate, stocks, art and investments.

ESTATE - think of it as another word for loved ones. Whatever you leave behind when you die; your assets less liabilities. Estate plans help everything go straight to those you love.

EXECUTOR - also called an estate trustee in Ontario. This is your estate's legal representative, named in your will if you have one or otherwise by the court.

GETTING PROBATE - going through the probate process when someone dies. Estate courts supervise what happens to estates and confirm your executor or estate trustee.

INTESTATE - a dirty word meaning you died without a will. The government then writes a will for you to divide your estate. A court appoints estate trustees from your family.

MARRIAGE CONTRACTS - legal agreements you sign before or during marriage to deal with family and estate plan issues. Also called the prenup.

POWERS OF ATTORNEY - you sign legal documents to designate agents for your finances and health care decisions.

PROBATE - a process that proves who shares and administers your estate. Probate or estate courts have jurisdiction over estates when someone dies with or without wills. Probate taxes are legally collected in every province but Quebec.

PROBATE DISPUTE - if you die without a will, a judge decides who your estate legal representatives are. If your will is contested, it can't be accepted for probate until a court settles the dispute. Loved ones wait and pay for the delay.

REVOKE YOUR WILL - canceling your will by your actions in destroying the will or by making a new will.

TAX ROLLOVER - a deferral of the tax of certain deemed disposition rules. Capital property left for a spouse or a spousal trust is a tax-deferred transfer.

TAX EXEMPT - assets such as insurance; includes a principal residence exempt from tax.

TRUSTS - are inexpensively created by your will and called testamentary trusts. Assets are controlled or managed for the benefit of trust beneficiaries like minors.

WILLS - legal documents you sign to deal with your estate. You appoint executors who manage and distribute your estate to beneficiaries after you die.

PERSONAL NOTES

PERSONAL NOTES

_____

_____

_____

_____

_____

_____

_____

_____

_____

_____

_____

_____

QUICK ORDER FORM

Fax Orders: (416) 769-9440. Send this form.
Email Orders: estatetips.com
Postal Orders: Mr. Wills Inc. c/o 62 Jane Street, Toronto, Ontario,
Canada M6S 3Y4

Please send the following books, disks, reports, or tapes. I understand
I may return any of them for a full refund, for any reason, within 30
days.

_____

_____

_____

Please send more free information on:

☐   other books   ☐   seminars/speaking

☐   consulting   ☐   audio or video tapes

Name: _____

Address: _____

City: _____ Province: _____ Postal Code: _____

Telephone: _____

Email Address: _____

Please add 8% sales tax and 7% GST to all orders.

Shipping: Please add $4.00 for each product in the same order.
Payment: Cheques, money orders payable to Mr. Wills Inc. or VISA
accepted.

Card Number: _____ Expiry Date: _____

Name on Card: _____

Signature: _____

QUICK ORDER FORM

Fax Orders: (416) 769-9440. Send this form.
Email Orders: estatetips.com
Postal Orders: Mr. Wills Inc. c/o 62 Jane Street, Toronto, Ontario, Canada M6S 3Y4

Please send the following books, disks, reports, or tapes. I understand I may return any of them for a full refund, for any reason, within 30 days.

_____

_____

_____

Please send more free information on:

☐   other books   ☐   seminars/speaking

☐   consulting   ☐   audio or video tapes

Name: _____

Address: _____

City: _____ Province:_____ Postal Code:_____

Telephone: _____

Email Address: _____

Please add 8% sales tax and 7% GST to all orders.

Shipping: Please add $4.00 for each product in the same order.
Payment: Cheques, money orders payable to Mr. Wills Inc. or VISA accepted.

Card Number: _____ Expiry Date: _____

Name on Card: _____

Signature: _____

ABOUT THE AUTHOR

Edward Olkovich is married and has two children. He has practised wills and estates law since 1978 in his Toronto firm. He is co-author of *Wills & Estates for Canadians* and author of *Estate Planning in Six Simple Steps for Canadians*. He has written for various publications including the American Bar Association and is regularly quoted in national publications. He is a frequent guest on television and radio shows on estate planning topics. As a lawyer, Edward is available to consult in the areas of wills and estates, including issues of capacity, estate administration and legal challenges to wills.

Edward has instructed new lawyers since 1990 in the Ontario Bar Admissions course. He has chaired various programs, sections and committees for the Ontario Bar Association including General Practice, Law Practice Management. He is an executive member of the Trusts and Estates Section and founding chair of Ontario's Make a Will project. Edward speaks at financial and continuing education programs, conferences and client seminars. His web sites include www.MrWills.com and www.Estatetips.com. He can be reached by email at edo@MrWills.com or by telephone at 416-769-9800.